I0103150

GOD'S CHOSEN WOMAN

Precious

A.R. Neal

Precious Media Group Atlanta, Georgia

All rights reserved. This book, or parts thereof, may not be reproduced in any form or by any means, electronic or mechanical without permission in writing the publisher

Copyright © 2015 by A. R. Neal

A. R. Neal

For more information about the writing of the author, visit

www.fallinginlovegodsway.org

ACKNOWLEDGEMENTS

Memories of Precious are not passing thoughts but are engrained in the hearts of her many friends and family.

To Mother Alice Banks my mother-in-law, Precious always reminded me, "That's my mama," when you treated me like your son. I thank you for being a God fearing mother who exemplified qualities that were reflected in Precious' character which were profound. I often wondered how Precious could treat me with an abundance of love, and then I recognized you possessed that same love.

To D. Elaine McNease, thank you for being my best friend, sister, confidant, associate, and editor. Without your support and dedication my efforts would be more difficult. I love you and thank you.

To Amanda Scott, thanks for your support and friendship. I appreciate your willingness to assist me.

To Beverly Gardner, my sister-in-law, I appreciate your support and encouragement. You have truly been a blessing to me. Thank you for expressing your unconditional love.

Last but not least I want to thank everyone who contributed to the publication of this book. Your expressions of the experiences you shared with Precious will inspire and motivate others.

TABLE OF CONTENTS

Preface   i

Introduction   iii

CHAPTER 1: Precious   1

CHAPTER 2: Unusual Kindness   17

CHAPTER 3: Living Sacrifice   26

CHAPTER 4: Living Testimony   42

CHAPTER 5: Unconditional Love   81

CHAPTER 6: Walked on Earth but Lived in Heaven   88

CHAPTER 7: The Beginning of the End   121

About the Author   167

Preface

This story is about a journey and not just a destination. Normally, when people envision a journey they instantly calculate it as time consuming. The first time Precious and I talked the Holy Spirit spoke to me clearly saying, "Things will happen not in man's time, but on God's time." The glory of God is definitely seen in the consummation of Precious' life. Our time together was short, swift, and captivating. When we just merely conversed it would invoked the presence of God. God spoke to me in so many ways during our union. He revealed things about Precious that she only spoke to Him. I laugh to myself when I think about how she reacted when she realized that God was speaking to me, as she would say, "about her business." She wasn't upset, but just shocked. It was truly amazing; we were so entwined that it was unreal. Thank God for choosing me as a witness to what may seem as a glimpse to some, but a life-time experience for me.

Introduction

When I first recognized her name as Precious my first thoughts were filled with euphoria. Her name not only brought joy, but I also thought to myself, "If her character reflects her name she is a gem." To my satisfaction her moral fiber exceeded every aspect of her name. She was a woman of excellence, beauty, humility, and love. I wondered about the origin of the name "Precious."

What is more, I also thought that maybe it was her nick name. To my surprise her legal first name was Precious. Furthermore, I later learned that the name "Precious" derived from the English word meaning, "Of great worth."

Precious displayed many extraordinary attributes. She was unusually kind to everyone and she met no strangers. Somehow she overlooked the negative in people and expounded on their positive characteristics. Precious taught me the benefits and blessings of being unusually kind. When I would say or do something that was abrasive or abrupt she would not chastise or criticize me, but just say,

"Unusual kindness honey." I would instantly pause then think about my ineptness and change my demeanor. I desired to give and receive love unconditionally long before I met Precious. I prayed that God would send me someone who would love me from the inside out. Not only did she possess unconditional love in our relationship, but she demonstrated unconditional love toward everyone she met. She helped others not based on their ethnicity, social or financial status, but because she shared God's love. When someone did or said something to hurt her she did not complain or retaliate.

Precious prayed morning, noon, and night. She was an intercessor and a prayer warrior. People would always call and ask her to pray because they knew she was anointed. I noticed that she did not mind praying, it was natural for her. She was a living sacrifice. Precious was always busy in ministry or helping others. While Precious never complained, her mother expressed concern to me about Precious not getting enough rest. She was only sleeping about three hours each night. For one reason, Precious was involved in several outreach ministries such as, prison and youth, she aided churches other than her own, she also fed and ministered to the homeless. Another reason is, Precious lived according to what she preached and taught. Therefore, her involvement in ministry was time consuming. Often times, people talk about how they love the Lord, but they do not reflect God's glory in words or action. Precious was truly a reflection; although, she was not sleeping very much at that particular time, she was about her "Daddy's" business and He gave her the strength and energy to complete her mission. Many questioned the validity of her faithfulness, but her lifestyle was untainted. When I share the story about my brief life with Precious, I am often told that, "she was an angel." I learned after her transition

that I was not the only person to have a story to tell,

but there were countless others with stories.

In the beginning of our marriage I wondered how

the consistency of her Christian life was sustained.

My question was answered when I saw a heavenly

countenance on her face two months before she

became ill. I noticed, although she was on earth she

lived as if she was in heaven. Her focus was to please

God totally and to let her light shine for others. I had

never been around anyone who exemplified a Christ

like life so genuine as Precious did.

I remember feeling so complete when we

married. I knew before I moved to Texas that my life would be transforming. I did not know that it would be the beginning of the end. There were many surreal occurrences during our brief courtship and marriage. I would tell my Sister and Pastor things that transpired. I recognize she passed a torch to me that I must pass to others.

CHAPTER 1

Precious

Her birth name was Delinda Fay Horton; she was born in Little Rock, AK on March 22, 1961. Delinda changed her name on June 23, 2006 to Precious Nafissa. I remember asking why she changed her name. Her reply was, "God changed my name." On the Testimony In Court — Adult

Name Change form, one of the statements says, "I am requesting the name change for the following reason (s): "Due to my spiritual and religious purpose/beliefs." Precious' response was sincere and direct. After hearing and reading her response I said to myself, "wow." My thoughts were short and simple only because I understood the magnitude of her name. Her awesome life-style reflected her name in every aspect. No doubt, it showed that she was truly a woman of God. As you will learn while reading about this remarkable woman, she truly lived what she prayed, preached, and taught. Her ministry was paramount in her life; nothing came before God. Her life exemplified sincerity, purity, and dedication. Furthermore, this is one way of defining her awesomeness. Most of her friends, co-workers, associates, and church members knew her as Precious not Delinda.

As an adjective, The *Encarta Dictionary the English (North America)* gives several distinct definitions of the word "precious." (1) *Valuable-worth a great deal,* (2) Valued- highly valued, much loved, or considered to be of great importance. (3) Not to be wasted- rare or unique and therefore to be used wisely or sparingly or treated with care (4) Used for emphasis—used for emphasis to express irritation, dislike, contempt, bemusement, or some

other strong emotion. (5) Fastidious or affected- too

carefully refine in language, dress, or manners.

The word "precious" truly expresses who she

was. When I think about Precious I am reminded of

how valuable she was, not in a monetary sense, but

in a spiritual way. Certainly, she gave

unconditionally of everything she possessed. She

welcomed the homeless to her home, gave food,

money, prayers, and her time to the needy. Many

treasured her prayers, opinion, and advice.

Precious, an important woman, was highly

valued and loved by countless confidants. Besides

that, she was so rare and unique that many questioned if she was genuine. Someone told me that some people would sarcastically make comments such as, "Is she real? I don't believe anybody can be that holy."

Yes, God used her for emphasis, she was not afraid to express irritation or dislike for sin. The devil was definitely bemused because she kept him bewildered with her passion and faithfulness to God. Her emotions in worship and prayer were overwhelmingly strong. Finally, she was fastidious or detailed; she did everything with perfection of God's reflection. She was very carefully refined in her language, she didn't use vain words, dress

inappropriately or display negative manners. In

essence, Precious was an extraordinary woman,

wife, and saint.

Many people view our love story as a fairy tale.

Surely, I don't have words to describe it other than

incredible and wonderfully blessed. We met on

October 8, 2010. We always told everyone that a

mutual friend introduced us. Of course, the mutual

friend was God.

During our first phone conversation I could feel

the power and presence of God penetrate through

the phone lines. In other words, I knew that

Precious was an anointed woman of God. I often laugh to myself when I think about her asking, "Can you pray?" That was one of the first questions she asked. I also laughed because I thought it was a silly question. Precious was testing to see if I had a prayer life and summarize my relationship with God. I laugh even more as I think about how the conversation ended. Precious stated, "You can pray now." As we prayed daily I understood the magnitude of having a divine prayer life. I was fond of her asking, "Can you pray?" I was also amused because she didn't know that I was a minister. For instance, after talking five minutes she asked if I could pray. Therefore, asking that question caught me off guard.

One of the first things Precious said, "I don't date." After making that statement and giving an explanation I understood clearly. Although our mind sets were similar, I still thought that dating to a certain extent was necessary in establishing a friendship relationship. I also felt that too much dating wasn't needed; especially, if a couple knows that God has ordained the dating relationship.

Precious stated that she didn't "believe in going out getting caught up physically, emotionally, and sexually." I admired her conviction. What is more, she explained that she raised her daughters the same way.

As I continued thinking I knew I could identify with her ideas and views on dating, but is she too radical; does she have a sense of humor? As thoughts continued to overtake me, I was reminded of two other women. These women had characteristics similar to Precious.' However, these were not lasting relationships. Consequently, I walked away. Whereas, after meeting Precious and continually thinking about her, it did not matter how radical she was or if she did or did not have a sense of humor. I could not walk away. One thing I learned about Precious after talking to her that first night was God was her first love!!!

I was at a place in life seeking more intimacy with God. I was living in sin filled with fornication and adultery; this led to a year of disappointed relationships. I returned to church in January of that year, which was 2010, but I sat in the back of the church. I asked my Pastor, Jamelle Mckenzie, whom I had previously served in ministry with, to allow me to just seek God. I had to allow the purification to take place in my life. It took several months but the process was life changing.

God emptied me; I didn't know it then, but I

later realized that God was preparing me to receive

His work with one of His chosen daughters. As

God sanctified me I lost my desire to fornicate, my

prayer life changed, my study habits increased, and

I even fasted more frequently. God even told me

not to work. I didn't understand at the time because

I only received commission pay. My finances were

nonexistent; I had very little food, and my rent was

past due. Now, I had to trust God completely. Only

two people knew my experience, my sister and

pastor.

As I continued to seek the presence and power

of God my desire to seek women ceased. Little did I

know that God had chosen me for Precious. After the first week we knew that God had joined us together.

While talking to Precious the second night the Holy Spirit told me to tell her, that our relationship "would not be on man's time but God's time." He said that, "things were going to happen quickly." Precious seemed precautious after hearing that; it was as if she didn't receive it whole-heartedly. I felt her reserve in my spirit and it didn't feel good. I can honestly say that was the only time that she ever caused me to feel that way.

Subsequently, God confirmed what He had

revealed earlier about the timing of our

relationship. One day Precious was talking to her

daughter and asked how her fiancé was doing.

Well, Precious kept calling my name (Neal) instead

her daughter's fiancé's name. This prompted her

daughter to ask, "Who is Neal?" After calling my

name several times she had to reluctantly tell her I

was a new friend. Precious' intentions were to give

our friendship more time before she introduced me

to her family and friends. When she told me what

happened I simply replied, "I told you what God

said."

From that point on our relationship transitioned

to a higher level. God spoke things in my spirit about Precious several times. As an example, we would converse over the phone and she would say, "Hold on a minute." After she kept telling me to hold I was curious. Therefore, asked, "Why do you keep telling me to hold on?" She plainly replied, "I'm asking my Father why He keeps telling you my business?" Precious knew at that point that God had chosen me for her.

So many walls came down the first month we talked. During that first week God also told me that I was her covering. As God spoke to me about Precious He had not spoken to me in that way before. We both knew that God had consummated our union. God entwined us to each other; because of this we were each other's supposed to be!!!

Although Precious was a very private person she shared things with me that she had not shared with anyone. She spoke of an incident where someone deeply hurt and took advantage of her when she was a teenager. I asked if she ever reported them, but to my dismay the incident went unknown until she told me. The only reason she told me was because we conversed about our first kiss.

I proposed to Precious at the end of October 2010. Precious answered "Yes" to my proposal.

Consequently, we tried to decide whether we would kiss in November after an informal ceremony or in March 2011 at the formal ceremony. Of course, I adamantly said it would be in November. This is when I asked why she wanted to wait. Then she stated that she had never "really been kissed." Precious explained that she had "smacked but not really kissed." This was a result of a ghost from her past. I must admit it was hard to believe. Given that Precious shared background information on some of her previous relationships, I knew her statements could have some validity.

CHAPTER 2

Unusual Kindness

Precious loved to read and study the Word of God. She sat up in her king sized, neatly dressed, color coordinated bed with her head propped against the head board and read or studied. I moved to Texas a month after Precious and I married; we prayed each night after studying. Certainly, she was more insistent than I was. I could be in another room writing or watching one of the local channels on television (we didn't have cable because Precious didn't watch television) and she would call me in the room and ask if I was ready to study.

One particular night I chose to study a Scripture in the book of Acts. I can't remember why, but I'll never forget the Scripture because it has a lifelong affect. The Scripture is Acts 28:2 (ISV) which states, "The people who lived there were unusually kind to us. It started to rain and it was cold, so they started a bonfire and invited us to join them around it." This Scripture exemplifies unusual kindness the islanders showed to Paul and the others that swam

to land after their shipwreck. They didn't know

who those strange people were that swam on

broken pieces of the ship and some on boards. Not

only did they welcome the foreigners, they kindled

a fire, and gave them shelter. No doubt, the unusual

kindness exemplifies the islanders. What is more, it

captured our hearts (Precious and mine).Thus,

Precious coined the phrase "unusual kindness,"

and from that day forward she used the phrase to

remind me if or when a situation would arise.

Precious reminded me because I was abrasive and

rough around the edges. On the other hand,

Precious was always unusually serene and celestial. In particular, if I said something out of the way or got out of order in a discussion Precious, in her sweet innocent voice would say very softly, "Unusual kindness honey." I didn't have to echo unusual kindness to her.

Precious experienced a conflict in her church, which truly troubled her spirit. This conflict may have caused gossip and discord among the church members; furthermore, it could have even caused the church to separate. Precious continued to serve as if nothing happened. She prayed and prayed for instruction and direction so she would handle the problem in a heavenly fashion. It was phenomenal how I was backing off and Precious was moving forward, I was negative and she was unusually kind toward the situation. Yes, God worked it out and resolved the matter in an orderly fashion.

Precious enjoyed walking, it was her daily routine to get up some days at five or six a.m. and walk around the park, which was about a quarter of a mile from our house. Before I moved to Texas she described the park over the phone. She stated that it was a "nice park, very beautiful and the track surrounds the water." I explained that it was not safe to go so early in the morning, but she responded, "Honey there are lots of people there in the morning and my Daddy (God) will protect me."

Precious was full of life and never met a stranger. She told me that one morning while walking she saw a man sitting and seemingly troubled. As they began to talk, she witnessed to him about God and salvation, (Precious would witness to a brick wall); he explained to Precious that he was homeless. Precious being the woman of God that she was, showed unusual kindness to a perfect stranger and allowed him to stay with her. A person's race was not important to her. In fact, this man was Caucasian, it didn't matter because she always looked at a person's heart. I don't recall how long the gentleman stayed in her house, but he received the Lord as his personal Savior.

This example of unusual kindness was heavenly and extraordinary; especially, since Precious was an attractive single woman. A couple of months after Precious told me that story, I asked what happened to the guy that she allowed in her home. She called and found that he was living in Houston, TX. He was a born again Christian, married, and working. We rejoiced while I inwardly couldn't believe she let a stranger move in her home.

Precious was a giver, she would give the clothes

off her back. She assisted ministries and helped start Non-Profit Organizations. Precious didn't charge anything for her services. Understanding the magnitude of the sacrifice she made one must realize that she was unemployed.

Thinking about Precious' unusual kindness is amazing because it was not about Precious, but the welfare of others. For instance, her mother told me that someone gave Precious a blanket; one day she saw a cold and homeless person and gave the blanket away. Precious was a very likeable person, but some people didn't like her. She was highly anointed and truly loved the Lord. In spite of how someone felt about her, she would extend unusual

kindness towards them.

CHAPTER 3

Living Sacrifice

One evening I was in one part of the house and Precious was in another. Suddenly, I heard a sound as if someone was talking or shouting. Precious was gravely sick, she could hardly walk, and the strength in her vocal cords seemed to diminish quickly. It was baffling hearing the voice streaming in the air. I thought to myself,

"This can't be Precious. She's so weak that surely her physical limitations won't allow her to communicate verbally in such a manner." I was curious and nervous as I left my desk in the office. Then I walked toward the living room and met this angelic type figure with hands lifted up and praying from the depth of her heart. Yes, it was Precious appearing as if she was not sick. I began thinking what's wrong with her? She should be in bed.

On the contrary, Precious was in prayer over the phone. I almost told her to get off the phone because of her condition. However, the Holy Spirit said, "Leave her alone." She continued praying for about fifteen minutes. I have always wanted to know who she was praying for that day. Be that as it may, this was the last person she prayed for before her transition to heaven. Furthermore, that was her last day on earth. I can imagine if everyone who knew or prayed with Precious would recollect, they would remember how detailed, extensive, and life changing her prayers were. Precious was a living sacrifice, and on that day she truly presented her body as a living sacrifice.

Granny, one of Precious' prayer partners, could attest to Precious' prayer life. Before I met Granny

Precious often spoke of her. She described her as a, "saintly motherly type who was a friend, confidant, spiritual adviser, and prayer warrior." She would visit Granny once or twice a week and take her food from the food bank. During this time they laughed, talked, and prayed. Granny lived about thirty minutes from Precious. I commended Precious for making the sacrifice and sharing her food.

Precious became unemployed in January 2010, but that didn't stop her from fulfilling her ministry call. Although she had limited funds for household expenses and gas for her vehicle she still made prison visits. Because of this, along with prayers

shared in faith, many prisoners got an early release

or reduced time. She would also correspond with

them through letters when she couldn't make a

visit. Some prisons were a couple of hours away.

While looking through Precious' papers I found

her ministry itinerary list for 2010. The ministries

are listed below:

Butler Housing Mentoring Program

Bible Study

Major event "Holiday"

Praise in the Park

Health Fair

Thanksgiving Dinner

Kingdom Building Prison Ministries

Kingdom Building Nursing Home Ministry

Dallas Baptist University (DBU)

Kingdom Building Homeless Ministry

Kingdom Building African (Hospital Ministry)

Gabon

Ministries/Churches Involved In

Precious Women Ministry —Watauga, Texas

Christian Love Family Church —Watauga, Texas

Set Free From Me —Fort Worth, Texas

Work Unlimited Partnership

Precious was faithful in giving her time in each of these ministries. Not only was this her ministry call, this was her life and purpose. Her life was a living sacrifice. In particular, she did not complain about how tired, frustrated, or disappointed she was.

One of the ladies who Precious coordinated the Bible Study with at Butler Housing told me an interesting story. She stated, "We had just finished Bible Study and it wasn't but a couple of people there and I was a little frustrated. Precious came out of the building praising God and saying, "Isn't God good? He had just who He wanted to be here tonight." I said, "We passed out hundreds of flyers where are the people?"

I found another letter that was seemingly written during Precious' first marriage. Based on some of the request listed, she called it her "Desire List." Looking at this list, it is easy to see where her heart was concerning her call as a servant. Of course, this is another example of how she was a living sacrifice.

Desire List

1. Walk with God and close relationship (know Him) Please Him and be in His will. Divine Plan

2. Walk upright

3. Bless others—Give out self, time, love, money, etc.

4. Husband—saved, love me as no other man can.

5. See understand and need God desire me for who the Lord has made me.

6. Be a witness and make a difference in many lives.

7. Job (good job) timing etc, glorify God in every expectancy

8. Director certification

9. Certified—training Aneb

10. Koinonia OFFE—Bless and go forth

11. Household fixed and furniture

12. All, every bill paid off, house, car, etc

13. Girls—Love of God, Godly friends

14. Church Lifted, Evangel Temple, witness to the world.

15. My sister needs and desires met

16. Pooh come home

17. Enhance my beauty, give me Christ love, be an encourager

18. Wisdom, Knowledge, and Understanding

19. Operate in all the gifts of the Spirit

20. Do your will in Saudi Arabia

21. The best racket ball in the world

22. Love

23. Love

24. Bless the Church

25. Let the street witness go forth and bless

26. Youth

27. 40 day consecration, be a blessing (see hear, listen, follow and do)

28. Pray and bless each person who is doing the consecration and give them direction

29. A mother —strength and finish blessing

30. **States her ex-husband's name here and writes**: to understand and see/hear what the

spirit is saying and even the letter change in him

31. Archie — car –growth

She then listed several other people that she prayed for and she ends by requesting

1. **To see the Kingdom of God move and forever**

As I read this list I mildly laughed to myself while thinking about the details and precision of Precious' prayers. At that point, I realized why she was so meticulous in her prayer life.

It was normal for us to pray before going to bed and upon waking in the morning. Precious had a special prayer life that I could not ignore. No doubt,

she prayed whether I prayed or not. For example, if

I was not ready to pray before we went to bed I

would hear or see her praying alone. The irony is

that she also prayed again with me. Nothing

hindered her from praying and she seemed tireless.

I was first in line of many that Precious prayed

with during the day. Precious and Mother Banks,

her biological mother, prayed everyday sometimes

several times a day. Precious prayed daily with her

two daughters. Additionally, countless others

called, and most calls ended in anointed, life

changing prayers.

On Tuesday and Thursday mornings Precious went to church for prayer service at 6:00a.m., but before she went she walked in the park. She faithfully attended the prayer service regardless of the lack of sleep from the previous night. I noticed when we met that she was getting only about three hours sleep each night. After Precious and I married Mother Banks would tell me that she hoped I would "influence Precious to rest more."

Fortunately, Precious began getting more rest. Her life was truly a living sacrifice and there was very little time for sleep. As a case in point, there was not much time left after ministry involvement, which included prayer, school work (part time), and always studying. In my opinion, one does not often meet a person who is highly anointed and angelic as Precious was.

I thank God daily for choosing and preparing me for such a heavenly experience. Precious wrote in one of her journals, "The weight of our walk should lead others to Christ." Sometimes I wonder how she did it. As previously stated, some people would make comments such as, "Is she real? I don't believe anybody can be that holy." Granted, I had firsthand experience with her; otherwise, I probably would have doubted also. The most important lesson I learned is we can truly be more than

conquerors through Christ when our life is totally

consecrated.

CHAPTER 4

Living Testimony

Precious' life was a living testimony. During our courtship and right before we married the Holy Spirit poured into my spirit to write "Falling In Love God's Way." Precious was excited because she wanted the book to exemplify a couple's conduct in relationships and marriages. I was also excited about the book. Most important, Precious was going to write final remarks at the end of each chapter. Unfortunately, she became ill shortly after I completed the first draft. However, she did get an opportunity to read it.

Precious and I agreed upon a chaste relationship. Though our courtship was brief it was tested the first week I visited her in Texas. This was a very challenging time since we knew that our union was ordained by God. I learned from this experience that as the Priest of my union it was my responsibility to display the up- most respect to my fiancé. My life had to be a living testimony also. Precious lives through me as well as through this book, just as she continues to live in the hearts of

the many friends and family members that loved

her.

We sat in one of her favorite Pastor's church one

Sunday morning. He exuberantly shouted to the

congregation, "Praise God like you are at a ball

game cheering for your favorite team." There were

two little girls about the age of four and five years

old staring at Precious with looks of curiosity as the

Pastor made his proclamation. Of course, Precious

began to shout Glory, glory, hallelujah, hallelujah

with all her vocals. Indeed, she already had a

surround sound praise. Because of this, the little

girls laughed mildly. I chuckled myself, not at Precious, but at the little girl's amazement. I immediately said to Precious, "Do you see those little girls laughing at you?" She sternly responded "I don't care the Pastor said Praise him like you are at a ball game!" Not only was her dedicated life a trademark, but most definitely her praise was.

Poo, Precious' nephew whom she was very fond of told his grandmother about the time he and Precious went to the mall. Precious told him to witness to people while he was there. When she returned she asked him, "Did you witness to anyone?" As Mother Banks and I discussed Poo's and Precious' trip to the mall, both of us agreed that she was somewhere witnessing after she left Poo.

Precious had numerous friends who realized she was a living testimony. I've lost contact with many of them. While reviewing some emails this particular one caught my attention.

She wrote:

"During the course of our lives we meet many people. Some of these people come to teach us lessons. Some come to test us. Some come to help us to the next phase in our lives. Some come for a short time and some come to stay awhile. Then there are those who come to go the distance with us, the ones who are connected to us in the spirit.

These are the ones whom God Almighty has put in our lives by divine appointment. Today, I want to tell you about such a divine appointment. In 1990, my ex-husband, my daughter and I moved to another air force base. I started attending a church there and ended up at a woman's function. There I met a woman named Precious. Immediately, we connected. It was as if we knew each other all of our lives. It was easy to talk to her and she actually understood me and vice versa. There were things I could talk to her about that I couldn't tell anyone else. She never thought I was crazy when I told her certain things and if you knew my experiences you would probably think I was crazy.

The amazing part of our meeting was that she was supposed to be gone already, but her ex-husband's orders got delayed. We didn't have a lot of time together before they left for their new base. I believe it was a couple of days later. Over the years we kept in touch, but sporadically. However, each time we did talk it was as if it was just yesterday. It was as it no time had passed. In the last year and a half we have kept in touch a whole lot better, with the last year talking almost daily. Any time I needed prayer she was always there for me. No matter what I went through she was there for me, while not passing judgment on me and vice versa. She loved God with all her might. She ministered to people in prisons, attended several churches, help empower young girls, and fed others who had less than she did. She did all of this with a not-so-good car, limited funds, and a whole lot of prayer. While she was not perfect, her love definitely covered a multitude of sins.

Last Thursday I lost my dear friend, Precious Bougrine, who was only 49 years old. Yet, in her young life she affected and helped more people than I can count. She is loved by so many, but I am ever grateful to the Father of all creation that He allowed me a chance to know her. I truly understand the relationship between David and Jonathan. It's nothing like having someone who knows you spiritually as well as naturally. Precious has taught me through her actions what it means to be a disciple of Yeshua the Messiah. Her love for God's people and Yahweh Himself was undeniable. I thank God for her life. While I am sad that I won't be able to talk to her I am extremely happy that she is where her heart's desire wanted to be —with the Father, who is in heaven. My prayer is that I too can do for the Kingdom of God as much as she has done."

Then she wrote a prayer.

"Our Heavenly Father, who is in heaven,

I thank you for my dear friend, Precious and the rest of my friends, whom you have given me. Please allow those who read this to have friends like I have. Thank you *for being wonderful and marvelous. I love you*

In Yeshua the Messiah's name, Amen."

She then gave Scripture references.

"A man that hath friends must show himself friendly: and there is a friend that sticks closer than a brother" (Proverbs 18:24, KJV).

"We are confident, then, and would much prefer to leave our home in the body and come to our home with the Lord" (2Corinthians 5:8, CJB).

"Therefore, stripping off falsehood let everyone speak truth with his neighbor because we are intimately related to each other as parts of the body" (Ephesians4:25, CJB).

"And now, Israel, what doth the Lord thy God require of thee, but to fear the Lord thy God, to walk in all his ways, and to love him, and to serve the Lord thy God with all thy heart and with all thy soul" (Deuteronomy 10:12,KJV)

More Testimonies From Friends:

Minister Bertha Samuels one of Precious' closest friends of twenty five years wrote, *"Mr. Neal Once in a life time, a true friend comes along they are someone you share your deepest secrets with, laugh together at life's treasured moments. Sometimes we laugh together for absolutely no reason at all. This person allows you to*

be you, so it is with Precious Bougrine-Neal. When I

think of her bubbling spirit, you can't help but smile

within. I truly was blessed to have known this Godly

woman, who enjoyed her Lord and Savior's life style, a

woman who enjoyed talking and praying daily. I thank

God daily for sharing in the rare gift of her friendship,

often a true friendship come once in a lifetime. When I

first met this woman, I had no idea that she would

impact me in such an amazing way, with her giving and

caring for others. Not until her departure you have no

idea how important this person is until they are no

longer around."

Minister Bertha Samuels-Turner

Minister Samuels-Turner also wrote a heart-warming memorial on Precious' facebook page: "As you, my friend, peer down from your Heavenly Home, I know my heartfelt thoughts. Thanks so much for 27 wonderful years of memories. I cannot express my deep sorrow at your departure. I think about you and he quite often and I remember many of our conversations and some of the words are still audible even now. During that time I had been bombarded with the passing of several loved ones, whose memories I will cherish forever. You have always accused me of having impeccable listening skills, but I believe that I missed 2010. You constantly reiterated how you felt about your imminent departure, in retrospect, there were many signs but I just didn't listen. I presumed that was something that would happen eventually, at some distant time.

I Just stopped by to say I miss my friend and co-labor in the

Gospel."

Another Person Wrote On Facebook: (Had not

talked in a while)

"How are you precious? Miss you pastor… and I

need your prayer all the time: love you so much!"

More Testimonies:

Sister Ruby Yavo, another dear friend and

fellow intercessory prayer warrior spoke these

words to me about her beloved friend. *"She was a*

prayer warrior, powerful woman, kind woman, faithful in going to prisons, and touched a lot of lives. When I went to the prison ministry with her I could see the respect they had for her. No one in the ministry is doing the prison ministry. Her life involved going in the world and ministering to people. She did a lot of things that she never told anyone. She was a prayer warrior, we were united and it still keeps me going. I would go with her sometime when churches would invite her to speak and pray.

Another dear friend who also became my close friend

Delores Robinson AKA Granny by those who know her:

Talking to Granny was the same as talking to Precious. Precious often told me about Granny during our courtship. I soon learned that they were seemingly cut from the same cloth. As Granny and I talked she reminded me and stated, *"I told Precious that the Lord was going to bless her with a husband."* *She said, "Precious was a very Christian and religious lady who really loved the Lord. She was very energetic and on the go for the Lord. She was always ministering to anyone that came across her path that's why we became friends. Precious and I would pray together she would bring me lunch, but we mostly prayed."* Granny and Precious have the same anointing. As a matter of fact, when speaking to Granny it's like being in the presence of an angel.

Mr. Ricky Fuller:

According to Mr. Fuller he met Precious over twenty years ago when she was operating her daycare. Precious told me about him and how good he was to her. One day Precious asked if it was it alright to have lunch with Mr. Fuller. I told her it was okay. That was the last time Mr. Fuller saw Precious. Later, I spoke with Mr. Fuller and asked if he would share what he remembered most about Precious. He was immediately filled with exhilaration. She left a life-long-long impact on his life. He and I had the same spirit of recognition about her life and character. I, like Mr. Fuller, have not met anyone as close to God as she was.

As Mr. Fuller began telling me about his friendship and life experience with Precious I could hardly write fast enough. Certainly, his words were motivational, exciting, and refreshing. Mr. Fuller said, *"Precious was all about God," and she told him that, "I am not going to put anyone before my God, if He takes me right now I'm happy." Mr. Fuller continued speaking, "Precious would never say no when he asked her to pray for him or anyone else. There was power in her prayers. I had a hernia infection I didn't know what to do, so I called Precious, she prayed and I never had the problem again. She was a great woman, always about God's business. She raised two Christian daughters. I am still amazed when I think about the impact she had and still has on my life. I don't just believe people when they talk spiritually but when I hear someone say I can't wait to be with my God, and I want to go home, like Precious use to say then I believe their walk."*

Another Facebook Testimony:

An associate of Precious wrote a note to me on face book,

"Precious and I worked together at one time. She was

a delightful person to be around. My heart went out to

her family when I heard about her going home to be with

the Lord. Of course, that is where we all want to go, but

she is missed here. She had a strong faith in the Lord and

she let the people that she came in contact with know

that. She did as our beloved Paul did by fighting a good

fight, finished her race, and kept her faith. To God be the

Glory!

Family Members:

As I talked to **Steven Flowers (Precious'**

Brother), he said, *"Precious was a true disciple of the*

Lord. She witness, evangelized, was a loving kind person

and was filled with the Holy Ghost. When I first noticed

her anointing was at a women's seminar I wasn't

supposed to be at in Geneva, AK. Even when we were

growing up she had compassion. She always showed

unconditional love, she valued nothing and whatever she

had she would give it to those in need. She truly showed

agape love.

Betty Flowers (Steven's Wife) also spoke highly

of Precious, "She was a very compassionate and

loving person. Precious treated everyone the same.

It was a blessing and privilege to have known her.

Dennis Horton (Precious Twin Brother)

passionately reflected on Precious when he said, *"I*

love her, miss her, think about her all the time, I wish she was still here, she was a good sister. She had a love for people that you can't imagine, she was a living witness, people knew she loved the Lord and she wasn't ashamed to witness. I miss seeing her, she was a good sister, good mother, she loved her mother and she kept her word. You can tell when she was around because you felt better. We all have to prepare ourselves like Precious did, so many of us forget that."

Archie Stewart (Precious' Second Oldest Brother) stated, *"I loved my sister, she was a sister, friend, and a good loving person. If you wanted to have a great sister, friend, or wife I would nominate Precious. If you wanted someone to tell you the truth even if it hurt* she would. She could be your sister, friend, or love you but she was going to tell you what's right and I liked that about her. I loved my sister but I knew she wasn't going to take up for wrong, she spoke her mind. She was a God fearing woman who was not counterfeit. I broke up with my ex-wife and I thought I broke up with my sister. Precious would give me a giddy look if I dated someone else. She told me I was wrong for breaking up with my wife and that I was going to miss her. She was right. Precious would give you her last and you would never know it but she wouldn't let anyone misuse her, she would tell you.

I went to prison for a year in 2006, I was about two

hours away from Precious, she would bring me ChickFil

A and would stay during the whole visiting hours. She

only missed coming to see me if my other sister came but

Precious didn't miss coming but a couple of times. She

didn't ride you but she made it very plain about how I

should do. When I was released from prison Precious

came and got me then took me to eat and asked me "what

was I going to do now that I'm out?" We went to the

social security office and to several stores. I stayed with

Precious and she was pretty stern about me not doing

certain things in her house. I couldn't drink my beer

although I would sneak some in the freezer in the garage

every now and then. We enjoyed each other; I remember

teaching her about football, I would be comfortably watching the game and she would come in the room and start asking me questions about the game. She would ask me to go buy her a large cup of tea from Quick Trip, we then would have tea and popcorn while watching the game.

Precious was one of a kind, everyone loved her from all races. Precious always told me that all you have to do is watch people and you will find them out. We were in Wal-Mart and Precious was talking to a homeless white lady and her kids from Houston, Texas. Precious asked me did I have any change and I told her I didn't. Finally she asked me to give her what I had so I gave her the ten *dollar bill and she gave it to the lady. One day we were riding and we went to the lady's house, I was surprised because the lady was homeless when we met her. Precious helped the lady get housing and she told Precious that the day they met, God told her she would meet somebody to help her. She was in an abusive marriage. The lady and her kids were hugging Precious and showing her lots of love.*

Beverly Gardner (Precious' second oldest sister) said, *"Precious wouldn't fight or argue with her siblings, she would just walk off. Would tell us if we didn't stop sinning we were going to hell!*

Mother Alice Banks (Precious' mother) said,

"My daughter was peaceful, she always tried to keep peace and she didn't argue. God always had His hands on her, she was a special child, and she was obedient and unique. She always wanted to serve the Lord. I remember when she and my oldest daughter went to visit a church and the Preacher was telling the congregation they needed to be baptized. Precious stood up and said she was ready and wanted to be baptized. The two sisters were baptized although they had been baptized. Precious' sister was upset because she had just had her hair fixed and she realized they had already been baptized."

A Pastor's Testimony:

Pastor Shun wrote a letter to Precious on

December 13, 2010 that was prophetic, personal, and anointed. This is what she wrote: *"Well hello mighty **Woman of God,** I haven't talked to you in a while I tried calling you but I got your voice mail. God put you in my spirit to speak to you personally but you must be at school, praying, or ministering. (Smile) I don't know what's going on with you but I'm sure it's nothing more than Spiritual Warfare in which we all are in so that's nothing new. I want to just encourage you and remind you that you are valuable to God and His Kingdom. Women like me need that wise counsel in our lives. Whatever storm you're going through right now just keep thanking Him and praising Him because he's* *still blessing you in your dry season. Rain is about to*

drench you Woman of God with a manifestation of major

blessings and major doors opening up for you in the

ministry. Wow what a mighty woman you are and your

husband, wow when you come as one what a powerhouse

you will both be together. Satan is busy, but God is also

doing some new things and doing some new

transformations inside of you and the first thing is

Patience! God gave me that word this morning. Romans

5: 3-5 and not only so, but we glory in tribulations also;

knowing that tribulations worketh patience! James 1:2-4

my brethren, count it all joy when ye fall into divers

temptations; your faith worketh patience. But let

patience have her perfect work, that ye may be perfect

and entire, wanting nothing. The Ultimate Test of

Leadership: The First of things to be changed is me the

Leader. The first order of things to be changed is Me,

THE LEADER. After I consider how hard it is to change

myself, then I will understand the challenge of trying to

change others. This is the Ultimate Test of Leadership...

by John Maxwell (Maxwell Meaning the Greatest). God

said, "Blessed is the man who perseveres under trial,

because when he has stood the test, he will receive the

crown of life that God has promised to those who love

him. Stop worrying about how you're going to fund your

wedding! God said, "I will send in a multitude of people

after my own heart to bless you!" Allow your faith to put the pieces together and continue to trust and have faith that **Nothing** *will stop the union. Watch God show up and show out on your behalf and expect a miracle and one of them is coming through one of your Daughters. I'm here Woman of God, I'm so happy for you and Pastor Neal! I know he realizes what God has truly blessed him with and that's a mighty Vessel of God, a major force to be reckoned with. You deserve all the happiness, Dr. Neal. You have a Doctoral anointing to teach and equip others! I love you so much and I'm sending my blessings filled with so much love and joy for you and where God is taking you, Dr. Apostle Neal! (Smile) I don't know if* *that's a combination to put together but you are Mighty!*

Walk in that dunamus Power.

Letter from DBU (Dallas Baptist University):

I was presented with a letter from DBU (Dallas Baptist University): "To the family of Precious Bougrine-Neal"

You probably know that the Dallas Baptist University 'family has been greatly saddened in learning of Precious' passing. I have visited with some of her professors through the day. I know that some will be attending one or the other gatherings/memorials for Precious. In that she is a "Ministry Student," it has been my privilege to have a few one to one visits with her prior to and during this semester, primarily on the

matter of the Grant and Scholarship we were pleased to

make available to her. She had a presence about her that

told me immediately I was talking to one who walked

closely with her Lord. Other professors have shared

similar observations to me of Precious. Not knowing the

family, I can only surmise the depth of sorrow you must

be experiencing. At DBU we have a wonderful Prayer

Ministry Office which several times a day sends prayer

requests out all over the campus asking for intercessory

prayer on various situations. The news of her passing

and the call to pray for you –the family —has gone out to

hundreds here at DBU. I have enclosed the original

document of Precious that is required for students

seeking the Grant. It is an account of her call of God to

ministry. I remembered reading Precious.' I was able to

locate it. I thought you might like to have it and let those

of your family read it. It will be a significant part of the

Godly legacy she leaves to all the family, especially her

husband, and children.

With our deepest Sympathy and prayers,

The Ministry Students Office, Dallas Baptist

University

Dr. Joe W Mosley

Ministry Students Dir.

After reading these testimonies from friends and family, one can surely say, Precious was a living testimony. Furthermore, she loved God and enjoyed her ministries.

I remember when Precious initially told me about her prison ministry. I thought to myself "what else does this woman do?" She was an intercessor, nursing home ministry, helped ministries start non-profit organizations, and helped organize ministries. She was as equally excited about the prison ministry and she gave one hundred percent of her effort. When Precious told me about the prison ministry I thought it was for women. I was wrong, she ministered to men. Besides that, the men highly respected her and desired her prayers.

Precious told me about early releases, prisoners who became Christians and began having services. Not only did she visit the prisons regularly, they also corresponded through the mail. Precious informed me that she didn't "allow any foolishness" in this ministry. She then proceeded to get the letters and said, "Honey these are the letters and you can read them." I didn't read them until after she transitioned. One thing I noticed most about her letters was the greetings began with

"Dear Pastor Precious." The prison ministry was a diverse group of men.

Precious' life was truly a living testimony. I remember someone telling me that some would question the validity of her faith, commitment, and love for the Lord. I mildly laughed when I heard those ridiculous comments. All the comments and letters about Precious have the same adage. I can confirm all of those sentiments. Although I lived with this woman of God briefly it was a powerful and life changing relationship. Yes, she was a praying woman; the first thing she did in the morning was pray and the last thing she did before going to bed was pray. She also witnessed

everywhere she went.

I went to a local food bank where Precious went

on occasions. I enrolled in a class there. This class

assisted people in finding jobs. After Precious

transitioned from this life, I saw the instructor of

that class. The instructor didn't know me or my

relationship to Precious. I asked if she remembered

Precious and she unsurprisingly did. Someone had

already told her about Precious and she was

shocked. The instructor talked about how energetic

and saintly Precious was. She left an impact at that

church and food bank. Yes I concur; she was a

great, powerful, God fearing woman, who is still

inspiring others through death.

CHAPTER 5

Unconditional Love

I took a picture of Precious and posted it on face book. I then posted the comment, "Beautiful!!!!!!!!!!!!!!!!!!!!!!!!" Precious wrote back "I will always love you!!! You are my gift from God!!!! Brason/Brazon/ Truly My Gift!!!! I responded, "Nothing can penetrate true love, it's God, and you two vs them!!! "Them" is every principality and power that tries to break down the wall of

oneness." Precious and I experienced unconditional

love in its purest form. Neither one of us were

perfect but we were perfect for each other. We

looked at each other through our spiritual eyes. She

once wrote me and said, "I love you, and loving

you, and in love with you." That blew me away!

Precious didn't do things for me based on

conditions, she just naturally reacted from her

heart. I tried to wash my clothes and she adamantly

refused to let me do so. She would say "that's my

role and you don't have to do that." She faithfully

cooked breakfast, lunch, and dinner until I told her

I don't eat that many times a day. At meal time she wanted me to stay seated while she brought the drink. She did those things unconditionally.

I refereed games in Capell, Texas on Friday nights. Precious faithfully traveled the hour and a half drive without a complaint. We left home at 4:30pm and arrived at the gym at about 5:45pm. I refereed five games and the first game began at 6:00 p. m. The building and facility was impressive and in a decent area. Nevertheless it was freezing. The air conditioner unit did not malfunction in the least. I wore a turtle neck underneath my basketball shirt; as I looked in the stands I could see Precious covered with her blanket.

Usually, during the first two games Precious studied her homework. After that she shivered the rest of the night, while trying to stay warm with her blanket, as she watched me run up and down that court. She traveled with me on three occasions. However, the last time I went to Capelle she didn't go because she was ill. Naturally, I missed her because we always laughed and talked on our way home; especially, about that cold gym. We usually arrived home around 12:30 a. m. Precious was so loving and giving, not just material things, but her unselfish concern for the welfare of others.

Significantly, she gave her time and all the genuine qualities of a generous woman of God. As an example, before her illness she was right there with me in that cold gym; she sacrificed giving me support as a loving wife.

So many people reminisced about how giving Precious was. She gave but didn't expect anything in return. I remember a friend called one day and he needed a ride to work because he had car problems. He lived forty five minutes to an hour away. Without a second thought Precious told him that he could get a ride to work.

Granny (as previously mentioned) is another

example, Precious faithfully took food to her from the food bank. Most important, Precious' love was not only for God, but she had an unconditional love for God's people such as Granny. Precious' love was so unconditional that she practiced unusual kindness in a way I haven't seen. People who offended her didn't know the extent of her offense. If correction was necessary Precious did it.

Precious taught me immensely what unconditional love requires. She mastered loving through pain. It didn't matter whether the person was a close friend, family member, or an associate, Precious loved them unconditionally despite intentions to mistreat her. No doubt, she always

resorted to prayer! I often said to myself, "How can

she still treat them with so much love?" Yes, she

taught me that unconditional love endures

regardless of adverse conditions.

CHAPTER 6

Walked on Earth but Lived in Heaven

1 John 2:15 states, *"Love not the world, neither the things that are in the world. If any man loves the world, the love of the Father is not in him"* (KJV). Precious' walk on earth exemplified the fact that this Scripture was an integral part of her life. I found some of her journals that dated back to the 80's and all expressed her love and commitment to

the Lord. Looking at some of Precious' writings I read two that that she wrote in 2010. The first one is a letter to Dallas Baptist University while seeking a financial grant in 2010:

"My personal call to a career in vocational Church related ministry is from the Holy Spirit and the Commandment from the word of God. Mark 16:15 (King James Version) "And he said unto them, Go ye into all the world, and preach the gospel to every creature."

My call to ministry is my life. God has place a desire and a passion in my heart to reach out to the lost, hurting, and dying world where ever I may go. He has also told me by his word Mk 16:15 (KJV) "And he said unto them, Go ye into all the world, and preach the gospel to every creature." I must obey my master with everything that's in me. I am compelled to do the work of my Father here on earth, even if it is only to make a difference in one person's life. I must be about my Father's business. I am called to work with women, men, boys, and girls of all nationalities. I feel an especially strong pull to reach out to women. Help by equipping them for the kingdom of God; by learning and studying the word of God, consistent prayer life, and obedient to his word. My heart is to follow Jesus steps; he went around doing good, by speaking life, healing hurts, and setting the captives free. My goal is to follow his *footsteps. Teach, and preach the gospel, and healing those*

that are hurting. I understand the pains of life, as a

single parent, God gave me the ability to raise two lovely

daughters who's serving God in a great capacity. I am

currently in a time of intense struggle, times are very

hard for me financially and I have been unemployed

since January 4, 2010. Nevertheless, God is in control

and has allowed me to complete the Advance Pastoral

Program at Christ for the Nations (May 10, 2010), reach

out to others and much more. There are times when my

faith is shaken to the core, but I continue to trust and

know that God is in control and will do just what he has

said. I am determined to walk as God directs me. This

time has helped my faith and has propelled me to move forward to the call on my life in reaching out to others. Doors are being opened for a prayer ministry, prison ministry, nursing home ministry, and a mentoring program to work with youth and their families in low-income housing. As I continually listen and walk in obedience God will lay out the specific plans of each ministry he's placing within my reach and hands that I may be about his business. Isaiah 42:1-15 & Jeremiah 1:4-5, 17, 19 "The word of the Lord came to me saying, "Before I formed you in the womb I knew you, before you were born I set you apart; I appointed you as a prophet to the nations 17 "Get yourself ready! Stand up and say to *them whatever I command you. Do not be terrified by them, or I will terrify you before them. 18 Today I have made you a fortified city, an iron pillar and a bronze wall to stand against the whole land- against the Kings of Judah, its officials, its priests and the people of the land. 19 They will fight against you but will not overcome you, for I am with you and will rescue you, declares the Lord."*

This is a powerful letter, Precious talks about her call, passion, struggles, faith, and journey. In essence, it explains her walk on earth while focusing on heaven. Her second writing dated September 27, 2010, which was eleven days before we met.

"My Life Mission Statement"

"My life mission is to see myself decrease and God increase as my unpleasant characteristics are crucified and transformed to the image of Christ to become a person of meekness with a quiet and gentle spirit, displaying love to my God, mankind, my family and to myself doing no harm. I will live my life according to the word of God so others may see Christ in my character, walking in strict obedience to the word of God and the laws of the land. I take responsibility for my actions to God, my community, church, job, family and the world which I live in, for what I do, what I say and where I go.

I want to leave an impressionable mark on the lives of

others through my character and life style that Jesus may not only be seen but he may be sought after with passion and fervor. My life will exemplify compassion for all people and a righteous and whole life style with God being the center of everything that I do.

I will give of my resources, such as my time, talents, and tithes, for the building of the Kingdom of God while reaching out to help those in need physically, emotionally, and spiritually. I will exemplify a faithful life journey that is pleasing to God and impact contagiously the people that are connected to my life. I will respect and honor my husband with my heart and action. I will listen attentively, praying for him and *doing good and not evil all the days of our lives. I will*

instruct and guide my family in the way of the Lord,

loving and cherishing who they are but giving them

room to develop into who God has designed them to be.

I will serve in areas that I am called to as Jesus

served. I will give of myself for the betterment of our

world, displaying and walking in honesty, truth and

compassion."

Wow, Precious accomplished her mission to the

letter, as she states her most astonishing attributes.

What is more, she recognized her imperfections

and crucified her flesh. Indeed, she allowed others

to see God in her, left an impressionable mark

through her astounding lifestyle; she respected, honored, listened, and prayed for me as her husband.

Pastor Shon Young wrote a memorial that completely describes Precious' walk on earth:

"Precious Memories by the Honorable Woman Of God! Heaven Scent her! Her Beauty Was Radiant! Her Presence was powerful! Nothing you ever seen before could compare to her. She was indeed a Virtuous Woman of God! She took being a Prayer Warrior and Intercessor for God to a whole new level that has not quite been obtainable by many thus far. I've never been able to quite put my finger on it until God called her home and I had

to sit back and think about the things that she would instill in me. It was definitely a Divine Appointment and impartation between God and Me through Precious! The things she would have me to read and research and send back to her for her class she called it proof reading but it was things that I needed to see and understand It was Wisdom. Everything about my Sister in Christ stood for excellence; she was a living example of how to live a Christian life being sold out only to God and not man. Her education and Knowledge of God meant so much to her she stayed in her books sharpening her skills because she wanted to know everything she could about God and how to please him and walk with him. She completed her race, she fought hard to accomplish the

ongoing ministry of Jesus Christ. Things that was shared

and loved by this Beautiful Woman of God was unseen

because she was beyond her years and not of the World.

So a lot of people couldn't understand her but I loved her

so much I embraced her Love and Dedication to God

because I want that same type of Love she shared for God

for myself. Her dedication to doing God's work lead her

on many journeys throughout her life which lead her to

eternity with God. I thank and Praise God for having the

opportunity to have such a Beacon of Light shine

through my life and she genuinely was concerned for my

soul and my walk with God through My Dear Sister In

Christ Jesus. We were more than just sister's in Christ

we was Best Friends for Life and I will miss her and

cherish the beautiful memories that we shared." By

Lashanda Young

Pastor Daniels' congregation wrote a resolution:

Resolution In Loving Memory of Precious Bougrine

According to his tender mercy, God, who is infinite in

his wisdom, has seen fit to move from our mist our

beloved Sister by means of death on February 17, 2011.

Sister Precious demonstrated a sincere and obedient

walk with God. She was a faithful member and Minister,

dedicated to spreading the Gospel. She traveled to far

places in outreach to help and deliver the word of God.

She visited jails, prisons, giving encouragement and

hope to the weary and lost. She also worked in the

community on many projects. Sister Precious was

accomplished in her education and until her death was

attending classes. Our beloved sister loved God as it was

evident of this in her praises to him. If she was ever sad

or worried one would never know for she had a

continuous uplifting word and praise on her lips. Sister

Precious touched many lives in different and special

ways. The family of Christian Love Fellowship extends

our prayers and encouragement unto the family of our

departed Sister. She will be missed but not forgotten. We

believe the words of Jesus in John 14 that encourages us

to "Let not your heart be troubled: ye believe in God,

believe also in me. In my Father's house are many

mansions: if it were not so, I would not have told you, I

go to prepare a place for you and if I go and prepare a

place for you I will come again, and receive you myself;

that where I am, there ye may be also."

Meet You At The Gate

A beautiful garden now stands alone, missing the one

who nurtured it

But now she is gone,

Her flowers still bloom, and the sun it still shines,

But now she is gone,

Her flowers still bloom, and the sun it still shines,

But the rain is like tear drops, for the ones left behind,

The weeds lay waiting to take the gardens beauty

away,

But the beautiful memories of its keeper are in our

hearts to stay,

She loved every flower even some that were weeds,

So much love she would plant with each little seed,

But just like her flowers she was part of Gods plan,

So when you hear it was her time he reached down his

hand,

He looks through the Garden searching for the best,

That's when he found Precious, it was her time to rest,

It was hard for those who loved her, to just let her go,

But God had a spot in his garden, that needed a gentle soul,

So when you start missing Precious, remember if you just wait,

When God has a spot in his garden, she'll meet you at the gate....

Humbly Submitted, February 24, 2011

Christian Love Fellowship Church

Bishop Louis Daniels, Co-Pastor Lady Brenda Daniels

The resolution dedicated in Precious' honor was powerful, truthful, and insightful. No doubt, she was a unique woman. Furthermore, she was exclusive, exceptional, distinctive, and rare. Granted, every woman is unique in her own way. I know that this woman of God was consistent in every aspect of her Christian life. She had class but wasn't high-classed. I often told her that she was "a girly girl." When she entered a room a gravitating glow appeared. She carried herself like a queen. In the same way, she treated everyone with equal amount of respect. She was exceptional or unusual in the sense that she lived what she professed.

Nothing or anyone was going to separate her from God. When I say that she was rare, I'm simply saying she was uncommon. She would often say, "I don't have time for foolishness" and she didn't entertain it either.

Precious' daughters often teased her saying, "You're having a Precious moment." Precious moments were those times when it seemed as if she was in another stratosphere and she didn't get overwhelmed about anything on earth. I quickly realized that things on earth went over her head. Someone may have spoken about her in a derogatory way, but Precious wouldn't flinch or show any emotion. I teased her saying, "Precious they are talking about you." She simply said, "I don't care; I don't have time for that foolishness."

The first time I noticed that she literally walked on earth and lived in heaven is right after an encounter I had with God. The first night after moving to Texas, I was awakened by a voice; I can still hear that voice today saying, "You are not going to have her long." "I asked what?" The voice then said, "She's not going to be with you long." Tears began to roll down the side of my face. Precious heard me crying and responded, "No honey we have ministry to do and I love you."

Three days later I saw Precious with a dazed look, it was as if she was here (on earth), but she was also there (in heaven). For three days I teased her saying, "You can come back down here with me now." She didn't respond. The fourth day the Holy Spirit told me to go and talk to her in a serious way. I went to her and I said, "You can go home to be with your Daddy." She repeated the response given on previous occasions, which was, "no honey we have ministry to do and I love you."

She was always thinking on those things above (heavenly things). So many testimonies about her always included how she loved the Lord and as Mr.

Fuller said, "she was all about God." She loved her

Daddy (God) as she affectionately called him. He

was the center of her life. One minute into our

initial conversation she asked, "Do you know how

to pray?" When meeting a new person, most people

try learning the person first, but she examined to

see if I knew how to connect with God! After the

first night of a long conversation she gently said,

"You can pray now." We conversed over the phone

for six and seven hours per night. I would go to bed

about five in the morning. I hadn't told her that I

was in ministry also. When I did tell her that I was

a minister she responded, "I am surprised that I

talked to you without knowing you were a minister because I was praying to meet a minister and I didn't verify that with you."

Matthew 6:34 states, "Take therefore no thought for the morrow for the morrow shall take thought for things of itself. This Scripture lived in Precious' spirit. As a case in point, Precious mentioned, "Having a lack of things was unfamiliar territory" to her, because she was accustomed to "the necessities of life." However, she didn't worry about the lack she suffered during the last year of her life. In fact, she didn't mope or complain. Surely, she just went about her Father's business.

Precious also mentioned certain injustices she received on her job. She was not exempt from jealous attitudes from co-workers. Although she performed her job at a maximum level she was unjustifiably released. God gave her favor during the last year of her life; she didn't beg or borrow but trusted God. I remember her confidently telling me how God had provided during her season of lack. For one thing, one of Precious' daughters supported her financially. Then another thing, Precious remained active in ministry, worked part time, met the needs of others, while God supplied her every need.

Meanwhile, Precious went to the food bank faithfully. The first time I went to the food bank with Precious I must admit a feeling of uneasiness. Personally, it was a humbling experience since this was virgin territory for me. My only experience was seeing people standing in a long line to get food at a church in downtown Atlanta. Now I was one of those who stood in a long line. It didn't seem to bother Precious, but I soon understood why it did not. First, we registered. Next, we sat in the sanctuary. Given that we were one of the first in line, our seats were on the front pew.

After sitting for about thirty minutes, I must

admit I was inwardly impatient. My mind was roaming with negative thoughts, why are they taking so long? Why are we here? And on and on my mind went. Then suddenly this tall, Caucasian, saintly looking man came to the front of the church. He began singing with an anointed voice. We began praising God as if we were at a regular church service. Some folks were just sitting and watching very emotionlessly.

I then realized that the main focus of food bank ministry was not physical food, but spiritual food. Precious and I were planning to have our formal wedding ceremony in March 2011. Our private ceremony was in November of 2010. After hearing

that man sing, "You Are So Beautiful," I told

Precious we must ask him to sing at our wedding.

After the praise service I asked the man his name,

he replied, "Tommy Lathen." This is when I asked

him to sing at our wedding; he agreed. We became

friends and I saw him when I went to the food

bank. The next couple of times I went alone. What

is more, I looked forward to going. Furthermore, I

enjoyed the praise service and the ten minute

sermonette from the pastor.

I learned something from Precious about this

Christian walk. One must not only talk the talk, but

walk the walk as well. She strived to do everything with perfection. For instance, one morning Precious and I were making the bed and I left some wrinkles in the comforter. Precious with her sweet, arresting voice said, "No honey you are supposed to get all the wrinkles out." I laughed and said, "Baby we are going to get back in the bed tonight." The following day I meticulous made the bed; when she came home from work I proudly told her, "Baby you didn't say anything about the bed." She responded, "Honey, I thought I made it up." I laughed to myself because I perfectly imitated her in that situation.

Precious was also particular about the food she

ate. In particular, she only ate chicken and turkey. I

told her if she ate my salmon croquettes that would

change her mind. Needless to say she fell in love

with them. One day I prepared salmon croquettes

for breakfast while Precious watched. As I put them

in my hand to make patties she quickly stopped me

saying, "Honey you are supposed to make them

neat and pretty." Yes, I slightly protested and said,

"We are going to eat them anyway." I then made

the edges perfectly smooth. Of course, that really

pleased her. I still find myself trying to perfectly

shape the edges of my salmon croquettes.

I believe Precious conquered many things, but driving is not one. A law in Texas prohibits drivers from talking on cell phones while in a school zone. Somehow Precious received a ticket because she didn't obey that ordinance. I teased her about her driving; especially, about her sense of direction. For instance, one day she and I had errands in different areas of the city. I must admit my patience was short. Precious gave directions which took us out of the way. In other words, we traveled unnecessary miles. Consequently, we doubled back to the point where we began. We didn't argue; however, I was slightly exasperated because I had been in Texas one month. Precious had lived there for a while.

Later I apologized for my lack of tolerance.

Precious also walked on earth but lived in

heaven in our marriage. At certain times she had

her "Precious moments." During those "Precious

moments" everything went over her head. Often

times I would react in a slightly cynical, but not

disrespectful way. At the end of the day, I

apologized to her. The irony is that she never

reacted, one way or the other, when I was

innocently abrasive. I think she knew my

personality. I prayed about it and the Holy Spirit

said, "While you are acting crazy she is praying!"

Precious was such a great wife that it prompted me to ask her, "How can you be such a good wife?" Her response was, "I have the ministry of a wife, and I am called to be a wife." Wow that blew me away. I knew God had truly blessed me.

Precious was a beautiful woman and her eyes were arresting. Men always approached and tried talking to her. One of her male friends often called for relationship advice. To illustrate, as we were walking on the track, this young man called, Precious told him to talk to her fiancée. I talked to him about his relationship issues and we talked a couple of other times. Precious met him in the post office several months before we met. I told

Precious, "That guy was trying to talk to you," she

responded, "I don't know what he was trying to do

I was talking about the Lord." Yes she walked on

earth and lived in heaven.

CHAPTER 7

The Beginning of the End

Precious and I planned to marry when I arrived in Texas. I flew to Dallas on November 22, 2010. Most important, we married that same week; we didn't tell anyone, not even our closest confidants.

I didn't have the nervous energy that one normally gets when meeting someone for the first time. Actually, I felt excited. Besides that, I began feeling impatient because we had communicated over the phone for six weeks and several hours a day. Now I could hardly wait to see my supposed to be, and my blessing sent from God.

She had an immense gregarious smile; I said to myself, "She is more beautiful than her pictures." Next, we greeted each other with a warm embrace. In the same way, we both smiled. Additionally, we laughed and talked about various subjects such as, her car, which was not running properly.

Precious lived in North Texas in an area called Watauga. I envisioned a lifelong union filled with years of sharing love and happiness. In contrast, it was the beginning of what soon was the end.

I spent the following couple of days getting acclimated to my new home. Yes, I was leaving Georgia and joining Precious in Texas. Precious and I were so in love, entwined by God and with each other. Chemistry between us was five times greater in person, which was especially important since we had only communicated over the phone.

No doubt, it was a challenge to control my flesh because my emotions were overwhelming. Of course, Precious' radiance was captivating. We promised each other and vowed to God that we would not have premarital sex. Yes, I must admit

A.R. NEAL

containing myself was difficult. However, I knew that she had a deeper respect for me, because I refrained from allowing my flesh to control me. We woke up early Tuesday morning and went for our marriage license. This was an exciting time because we knew God had ordained our union.

Our next challenge was to inform Precious' mother, Ms. Banks, about our marital plans. Therefore, we drove to Little Rock, Arkansas on Wednesday morning. I remember laughing and talking. All of a sudden I quoted lyrics to a song about Precious. Indeed, the lyrics were divinely given to me,

"You enter into my heart; you are my gift from God.

My love was captured by your spirit, which make it so

easy to write these lyrics, I never thought this could

happen to me, A perfect woman of God I truly see,

Thoughts of you stay in my mind, another like you

would be impossible to find, Only because God gave you

to me, because of this we know it's supposed to be, I love

you, I love you not in a world's way, God's spirit

entwined us in His own way, Your love for God grows so

deep I must stay connected to Him if you I'm to keep."

At this point Precious became silly and wouldn't

be quiet. She was laughing while she was writing

the lyrics. Given that I was upset, I told her that she

was "messing up my flow." At this point, she was serious again, but I would not quote anymore words to the song. On a couple of occasions Precious asked me to finish the song, but I never did. She even sent me an email with the words. Moreover, at the end she wrote, "(This is where you ended, God please give him the flow back to complete this song, thank you Father)." I didn't add anything else; as I read it later I realized the song was complete.

The drive to Little Rock, Arkansas from Watauga, Texas was about five hours. We stopped a couple of times, once for food and also to let Snow

(Precious' dog) roam around briefly. Snow is a very beautiful show dog with totally white hair. In addition, he is very smart. Precious was leaving Snow in Little Rock with Ms. Banks for a while.

Although Snow was adorable, I was not enamored with him as everyone else. My problem was not Snow. I concede that my mind set was not to care for a dog. Precious and I agreed and understood that Snow was her total responsibility.

When we arrived at Mother Banks' house, she was pleasantly receptive. She and I talked as if I had been in the family for years. Mother Banks politely allowed me to occupy her bedroom for the next three days. As I observed this mother and

saintly woman of God it was obvious that Precious

inherited her core traits from her mother.

Mother Banks prepared my food, drink, and

whatever I needed. I was not allowed to serve

myself in any manner. The aroma filled the house

with a pleasant smell of prepared food for the

thanksgiving banquet. As I observed the prepared

feast, I noticed there was no potato salad. Indeed,

potato salad is one of my favorite dinner side

dishes. Therefore, I asked Mother Banks, if she was

preparing this dish.

Precious teased me about "bothering her mama

about some potato salad," but Mother Banks

ignored Precious' comments and said, "I'm going to

make some potato salad." I just smiled and enjoyed

our visit. The ambiance of the occasion was

exciting. Especially, since I usually spend holidays

alone.

As I have mentioned Precious and I had a

challenge. In particular, we wanted to inform her

mother about our marital plans. However, the idea

of getting Mother Banks' approval was

intimidating. Although Mother Banks is kind, easy

going, and loving, she has a certain awe that breeds

accountability. In a like manner, this was as

intimidating as asking a Father to receive his daughter in matrimony.

To this day I don't know why I abruptly asked Mother Banks to meet with me without Precious. We met in the bedroom; I told her our plans, gave her my background, and then asked for permission to marry her daughter. After approximately a one hour discussion, Mother Banks stated, "You are not going to just be my son-in-law, but you are my son too! From that day on our relationship has been impeccable.

Precious was absolutely shocked that I conferred with her Mom without her. Be that as it may, it was exciting because now I had blessings from a woman whom I highly respected. Furthermore, I gained this respect over a short period.

After a pleasant three days in Arkansas, we left around 4:00 a.m. Saturday morning. The excitement and happiness we shared were blissful. Then we traveled to meet Bishop Daniels to join us in holy matrimony. Precious and I arrived in Texas around 3:00 p. m. we met Bishop Daniels, his wife, and daughter around 4:00 p. m. and he performed the ceremony. Bishop Daniels pronounced us husband and wife. As a result, we began planning a formal celebration with family and friends. This was truly the end of the beginning.

I returned to Atlanta on Monday morning November 29, 2010 with excitement. I wanted to tell the world that I was married. The only person I told was Delores McNease, my sister. My life was changing forever and I was not apprehensive in the least. It didn't matter that the only place I had ever lived was Atlanta, Georgia, or we had known each other for only seven weeks before we married. Little did I know that time would become an important factor in our union.

As I prepared for my new location, I suddenly realized that my son and daughter would not understand my plan to move. Besides that, Precious

wanted us to spend Christmas together, but I told

her it would probably be a day or two later. Yes, she

prayed and I was there on Christmas day. My son

helped me move a desk and he saw all my things

packed and I told him I was moving to Texas. He

told my daughter, she was upset. I left Atlanta

around 3:00 a. m. and arrived in Texas around 3:00

p. m. First, I noticed how large the state is; second

the traffic was worse than Atlanta.

As I arrived, Precious and I felt a welcome rush

of excitement. Moreover, love and joy filled the

house. The next morning around 6:00 the Holy

Spirit woke me up. He stated, "You are not going to

have her long," and I said, "What," He spoke again,

"She is not going to be with you long." Tears ran

down my cheeks and I cried verbally.

God is so awesome; although, He values our

time in this world He does not measure time.

Certainly, to Him one day is as a thousand years.

For example, 2 Peter3-8 tells us, *"But, beloved, be not*

ignorant of this one thing, that one day is like a thousand

years, and *a thousand years like one day"* (KJV).

Yet, many live each day carelessly without

regards for seeking heavenly things. Additionally,

the next verse states, *"The Lord is not slack concerning*

his promise, as some men count slackness; but is

longsuffering toward us, not willing that any should

perish, but that all should come to repentance" (v9).

This Scripture is of special significance to me; especially since the Lord prepared me for Precious' imminent departure. After telling me, "You are not going to have her long," I must admit my concept of longevity was much longer than it actually was. In particular, the four months and one week that I knew her seems like forty years of loving experiences.

We didn't travel as planned, we did not celebrate our first birthday together, we did not meet every one of each other's friends, and she and my family didn't meet in person. Seemingly, we had many voids. However, loving her and receiving her love from within canceled all voids. I will always treasure the last two months of our lives together. January and February of 2011 Texas and other areas of the country experienced heavy snow storms. Because of this, we enjoyed our time of bonding and intimacy.

Given that our finances were low we survived. I began refereeing basketball games and I was doing very well. Furthermore, my reputation as an official was growing and I was refereeing several days a week. Precious was substitute teaching at local elementary schools, which kept her busy. In spite of our lack God still provided.

On our first date I took Precious to Texas Roadhouse. After that we planned date nights. Thus, on our first and second date night we went to Texas Roadhouse again. Even though Precious only ate chicken and fish, she insisted upon going back to my favorite restaurant. Texas Roadhouse had a chicken dish on the menu that she enjoyed.

On our last date night Precious wanted to go to Baskin Robbins. She wanted ice cream. What is more, she had coupons. At that time I had a problem with a cavity. Therefore, I was hesitant at first. However, I did yield to her request. I remember her excitement about getting, what I was thinking to myself, "some ice cream." The coupons were "buy on get one free;" we each had our own. Little did I know, this was our last date night. I now realize her excitement was more than just ice cream. She was excited more about me honoring her request. More importantly, I feel somehow she probably had a premonition of things to come.

Precious was a very special, highly anointed woman of God. Before meeting her, my spiritual life consisted of highs and lows. I experienced a divorce in 2001, which was difficult because I have always been the marrying type. Meeting women was not a problem. Of course, the most difficult for me was meeting the right one.

About three months before I met Precious the Holy Spirit told me to quit my commissioned paying job, study, pray, and fast. This was the final stage of my purification and preparation for the blessing God had prepared for me.

During the previous several years I exiled myself from ministry. As a result of preparation and restoration, I reconciled to God during the early part of 2010. I cautiously worshiped Him with sincere awe. As I have mentioned, I sat in the back of the church. I did not preach, pray for anyone publically, or do anything actively, but praise God.

God prepared me for a life-long committed journey with Him and an anointed woman named Precious Bougrine. Precious did not desire a perfect man; she just wanted man whose heart was after God's heart. Although she was an intercessor and prayer warrior, during our prayer time together, I led prayer most of the time. Of course, Precious always prayed heart-felt powerful prayers.

Everyone Precious prayed with noticed that her prayers were unique. In fact, she received calls daily with prayer requests. My prayers were much shorter than hers. Nevertheless, she didn't make me feel that her prayers were more efficient. That woman lived in prayer, she literally prayed in her sleep. We prayed every night before going to bed, and every morning after waking up. Some mornings Precious woke up before I did. I could hear her in the bathroom. After she finished she returned to the bedroom, kneeled on the side of the bed and prayed. I would lie there and meditate while she prayed for thirty minutes to an hour. When she finished I said "Good morning" and she asked, "Are you ready to pray?"

Sometime I still laugh to myself when I think about some of her habits. Perhaps, many people thought they were abnormal. Our last prayer, before her illness, was very special; we knelt together on the side of the bed. I led the prayer that morning and it lasted about fifteen minutes, when I finished Precious prayed. She didn't normally do that. She began at 8:15 and ended at 9:10. This was another sign of the beginning of the end. Everyone and every situation that entered her spirit were covered in that prayer. Granted that I teased her quite often, I didn't cross the line with her prayer life.

Precious' faith was a strong, she didn't waiver or doubt God's omnipotence. Moreover, I only saw her show weakness twice. She was so closely knitted to God that people needed to see her human side. There were two distinct times that Precious solicited my prayers. I am reminded of how she emptied herself to others. In the same way, she requested this from me.

Those two occurrences reminded me of Jesus in the Garden of Gethsemane. He was deeply grieved and distressed even to the point of death. Jesus began praying for deliverance from the trials, death, tribulations, expectations, and fears. This was his flesh, his natural man speaking. According to the Gospel of Matthew Jesus said, *"Yet not as I will, but as you will"* (26:39b; NASB).

Precious asked me on those occasions, "Why, I've been faithful?" She cried and I prayed. There were countless times that I led prayer, but those two times the anointing of God was in that house; more than I had ever seen. We were almost powerless and it seemed as if we were in a trance. Now I realize that was also the beginning of the end.

It was February 16, 2011 at about 9:00p.m. I was in the office writing, and I heard a loud noise.

Precious was in the bedroom resting and very weak. The noise concerned me because I knew it could not have been Precious. As I left the office and walked in the hallway, there was a remarkable sight. Precious was praying one of her boisterous prayers. As a case in point, one hand raised to the sky and the other hand on the phone. I thought to myself, "I need to tell her to get off the phone because of her health." The Holy Spirit spoke and said, "Leave her alone." that's exactly what I did.

I went back to the office and she kept praying. I don't know who she was praying for, but this was probably the last person she prayed for before her transition. She transitioned the next day. Precious

refused to see a doctor. She adamantly responded,

"They can't do anything for me." However, we

discussed and agreed that she would see a doctor if

she didn't feel better the following day. This was

another sign of the beginning of the end. In other

words, she was trying to tell me her journey on

earth was near the end. I totally missed the

revelation intended for me.

On February 15, 2011, two days before her

departure, Precious approached me with this

statement, "You haven't sleep in the bed with me

for over a week." I quickly responded, "Baby you

GOD'S CHOSEN WOMAN PRECIOUS

are sick and it doesn't make any sense in both of us being sick." She responded with words that remain in my mind, "Honey you are supposed to love me." That was a powerful statement; it exemplified the meaning of the marital vow phrase "In sickness and health. That night my intentions were to sleep with my wife, I opened the bedroom door and immediately I felt humidity on my face, Precious was cold natured; therefore, the bedroom was always extremely hot. Precious was studying. For this reason, books were all over the bed. I closed the door, went to the other room and slept. I had no idea that it was her last night in the house.

During that time, Precious' oldest daughter was coming to town in a couple of days. Given that the shower did not work, I needed to go to Home Depot to get the fixtures needed to repair it. Of course, I wanted Precious to go with me, but she didn't want to go. That was unusual because we were always together. Although she could hardly walk I finally talked her into going. Her steps were very slow and deliberate. While walking in the store I saw her literally hold herself up as she leaned on the buggy.

Even though, Precious didn't feel her best she excitedly asked me with her sweet gentle voice,

"Honey do you want me to buy you lunch?" Then she said, "I'm going to buy you lunch." This was our last supper together, the beginning of the end.

I repaired the shower the day before Precious' daughter arrived from out of town. Further, I cleaned the house, and washed my car; then, around 3:00 p. m. I heard a voice say, "Stop what you are doing and go lay with your wife." I went to the bedroom and lay in bed beside her. Next, I massaged her body. She was extremely sore. In fact, she could hardly bare my rubbing against her body. After lying in bed about fifteen to thirty minutes, I asked if she wanted me to fix her a nice hot bath with Epsom salts. She said "Yes."

After I prepared the bath water we got clean pajamas for her to wear after her nice warm soak bath. Precious could barely lift her legs over the top of the bath tub. This was very difficult for me because I was emotionally feeling her pain.

Finally, she got in the bath tub and relaxed. Then I said, "Baby you know that I love you, and I won't trade you in for a Mercedes Benz." She looked at me with a faint smile. Indeed, the pain was so intense that she could not even laugh. Then I continued, "If I have offended you in any way I am sorry." She just looked at me as if to say, "Okay."

After that, I told her I would be back in a minute.

When I returned another sign of the beginning of

the end occurred. Her end was near. As I walked in

the bathroom Precious was making convulsion like

noises. I ran to the bedroom and dialed 911. We did

not have a cordless phone; therefore, I stayed in the

bedroom. This was very difficult because I thought

her end had come.

I informed the 911 operator of the emergency;

she responded, "Someone will be there shortly."

My task was dressing Precious before the

paramedics arrived. It took about five minutes to

get her into the bedroom. Then I said to her, "Baby

you have to hurry up, I don't want those men

(paramedics) to see you naked." She abruptly

responded, "I am not thinking about those men!"

The irony is Precious showed more strength

putting her clothes than she had shown the whole

day. I still smile when I think about that moment

because I realize she did it for me.

The Holy Spirit gave me another revelation

about her convulsion experience in the bath tub. He

said, "She was not convulsing, but speaking in

tongues asking me if she could have a little more

time to see some people before she departs."

Precious' brother-in-law confirmed this revelation

during the eulogy saying, "Precious actually was supposed to die in the bath tub."

The paramedics arrived; as they prepared to transport Precious to the hospital, they asked if I wanted to ride. I said, "No," because I needed transportation back home. I had to map quest the address. I arrived at the hospital about 5:30 p. m. The doctor was examining Precious, and the nurse came out to speak with me confidentially. She said, "I don't normally tell the family personal information, but if you have any relatives that want to see your wife you need to call them."

As I reflect on the moment the nurse spoke, I

was devastated by the impact of the news. No

doubt, my feelings were somewhat ambiguous.

Although I understood what she said, mentally, my

mindset was not in sync with what I heard.

Immediately I called several people, Precious'

mother, daughter, and sister. Meanwhile, I went

back to check on Precious. She gave me another

sign of what was the beginning of the end. She

instructed me to call Pastor Daniels, Minister Bertha

Burke, and her daughter.

Precious' oldest daughter, sister, and brother-in-

law came around 6:30 or 7:00 p.m. Bishop Louis

Daniels, his wife, and several members of his

congregation arrived around 8:00 or 8:30 p.m.

Certainly, joy, hope, and prayer filled the room that

evening. There were not any feelings of trepidation

in the room, Precious talked and smiled; she

seemed peaceful. Personally, I felt that things were

now okay and it was just a matter of time before

things were normal again. Eventually, everyone left

the hospital around 9:30pm. Everything was fine

until about 10: 30 p.m.when Precious' health

spiraled downward again. The nurses administered

flawless attention to her as she lay there in horrific

pain, with several tubes connected to her body. The

ambience in the room was the exact opposite from

the previous hour, I was now more apprehensive

than ever. As time progressed I helplessly watched

the nurses attempt to raise her blood pressure level.

Meanwhile, all Precious and I could do was pray.

Pain saturated my heart as I watched my wife, love,

best friend, and spirit mate suffer. She had not slept

all night and I knew she would stay awake as long

as I was with her. Therefore, I left the room.

I left the room around 3:00 a.m. I called Precious'

mother and my sister. After talking to them briefly I

went back to check on Precious. As I looked in the

room about 3:15 a.m. Precious was turning over

and resting, I did not disturb her. I planned to rest

in the waiting room on the same floor, but there wasn't much space. For this reason, I went downstairs and slept in another waiting room. I woke up about 5:25 a.m. and went to Precious' room only finding the nurses rushing towards me saying, "We have been looking for you, your wife passed about thirty minutes ago." I did not get excited nor did I cry, but I had an epiphany and I understood. This was the end of the beginning, because now she was with her "Daddy" in a place where she always strived and longed for.

The church members, friends, and family were in a state of shock. Precious did not have any major health problems although she went to the hospital a

couple of times for blood pressure problems. At

that time her blood pressure was high, but this time

it was too low.

During the next couple of days much of the time

was spent planning her home going. We made a

decision to have two home going services, one in

Texas and the other in Arkansas. The wake was

held at Christian Love Fellowship in Watauga,

Texas, and her Home going service was held at First

United Methodist Church of Watauga because the

sanctuary could accommodate the attendance. Her

second service was held in her hometown in Little

Rock, AK. Hence, two people gave their lives to the Lord.

If God approached me today saying, "I'm going to send you through the same experience again with the same results," I would say, "Okay Lord here I am."

As I conclude this amazing semi-biography of this wonderful, powerful, anointed, loving, and sacrificing woman of God. I thank God for allowing me the privilege to experience Him through her. We had an intimacy that existed and exceeded a normal physical familiarity. We were truly entwined by God and with each other. Our love could not be measured by status, but was knitted

through Christ. Our union was brief, but extensive;

puzzling to some; full of clarity to me; envy by

some; elation by others; guilt for some; and

innocence for others. I understand that some people

disagreed with our marriage. In fact, that's been

obvious since her transition. I can only pray for

those who harbor ill feelings. Precious and I were

one, when she hurt so did I. We had one thing in

common, which was shielding pain. Above all, she

did that well her last couple of weeks on earth. She

had so much going on and some things she just did

not want to face unless absolutely necessary. She

was an inspiration when showing me how to display unusual kindness.

We met in October 2010, married in November 2010, and she transitioned February 17, 2011. We planned to start a couple's ministry. I also completed our book, *Falling in Love God's Way* two weeks before her transition. The morning I told Precious about my revelation to write the book, *Falling In Love God's Way* (FILGW) she felt elated. In addition, she was even more ecstatic when I asked her to write a summary at the end of each chapter.

Unfortunately, due to the end of the beginning, time did not permit her to give her input. However, she did read the first draft. The birth of Falling In Love God's Way (FILGW) Organization is a result of our marriage, which God ordained. Precious and I envisioned this organization as an example of our chaste relationship. In particular, the writing of *FILGW* serves as a guideline for others falling in love. *FILGW* serves as the foundation for readers in their quest for loving, productive relationships, and marriages.

My life has truly become the end of the beginning. I am commissioned to carry the torch that Precious passed me. The torch has been heavy at times and many times I've called her name and said I can't do it the way you do. I am always reminded of that voice inside me that says, "I sent you to her to show you that you can do it."

The many posted testimonies, letters, and interviews about Precious all speak in the same tone. She loved God, would give her last, gave of herself, and would tell people if she felt they were wrong. I remember her getting on my case two days before she transitioned. We planned a formal wedding for March 2011; we were truly blessed with the favor of God. Friends were supportive donating their services and assistance. Although our expenses were minimal I still felt that we needed to wait. Precious boldly proclaimed,

"Where is your faith?" "You are supposed to be a

man of faith!" After seeing her faith, I responded, "I

have faith and we will have it in March." She then

asked if I could have $1,500.00 by March, I said,

"Yes." Precious did not waver her faith. I thank

God for the ability to give her the love she desired

from her husband. I now realize that God chose me

for her.

During my stay in Texas, I met Mike Rush in

Dallas, Texas and we became friends. He told me,

"God would not bless me with her if He didn't have

a greater life for me." I did not understand at the

time, but now I do.

One of Precious' childhood friends wrote me shortly after Precious transitioned and said,

"Regarding you the one she talked about so quickly that day; she spoke with confidence that you were God's blessing for her and talked quickly about how sure she was. Then she had to go on with her business, but said she would call and tell me more." Precious went on with her business, her **Father's** business.

When Precious and I met this was the beginning of the end, and now that she's gone it's the end of the beginning. God already knew the end from the beginning. As a matter of fact, God knew and revealed the end from the beginning of this

wonderful, precious relationship. Isaiah 46:10

explains it perfectly, *"Only I can tell you the future*

before it even happens. Everything I plan will come to

pass, for I do whatever I wish" (NLT).

Precious your love is shared by many; we love

you, and miss you. Your legacy will live eternally.

Your Supposed To Be, Neal

About the Author

A. R. Neal, known as Neal by most, started writing poetry while in elementary school. A talent he inherited from his mother Ms. Ruby Neal, who still wrote poetry until she passed away at the age of 92 years. Neal was inspired to write his first book in 2006, which is entitled, *Am I A Man?* It is based on life lessons he learned on what it takes to be a mature husband and man. The lesson occurred after experiencing a life altering divorce.

Neal was inspired to write his second book, *Falling In Love God's Way*, during his whirlwind courtship and marriage to Precious Bougrine Neal. It is based on their spirit-filled romance and matrimony. Neal's third book, *God's Chosen Woman, Precious*, is based on a semi-biography of his wife. Precious lived a life totally dedicated to serving God and everyone she met; she had an angelic spirit. She valued motherhood, marriage, family, and most of all her relationship to God. She taught me the true meaning of being in the world, but not of the world.

Neal is a native of Atlanta, GA; he attended

David T. Howard High School and Morehouse

College. He is an ordained minister, motivational

speaker, poet and writer. Neal is thought of by

many as being humble, genuine, straightforward,

loving, charismatic, chivalrous, and God fearing.

He has a daughter Maranda Neal, a son Jason Neal

who are both college graduates and a

granddaughter MaCaylee Neal-Stembridge.

www.ingramcontent.com/pod-product-compliance
Lightning Source LLC
Chambersburg PA
CBHW071222290326
41931CB00037B/1857